ETERNALLY EXPECTING

DISCUSSION GUIDE

by Amy Liz Harrison

A Mom of Eight Gets Sober and
Gives Birth to a Whole New Life...Her Own

alh

AMY LIZ HARRISON

About the Author

WELCOME

By Amy Liz Harrison

Amy Liz Harrison is a bestselling author, podcaster, and mother of eight who writes books for both kids and adults. Sober since 2011, Harrison's memoir series takes an honest look at her past drinking and road to recovery, her diagnosis with ADHD as an adult, and navigating life as an unapologetically awkward person.

Her decades of experience parenting through adversity inspired her to create a kid's book series about mental health. A former high school English teacher, she holds a Bachelor's in Communication from Azusa Pacific University and lives with her husband, who she married in 1998 after knowing him for five months, and their brood in Bellevue, Washington.

also by the
Author

While *Eternally Expecting* navigated the bumpy ride of Harrison's early adult life, Eternally Awkward takes the reader back to where it all began! Before she was the quirky mom of eight, Amy Liz Harrison was a California kid, growing up in the 1980s, obsessed with Madonna and Moonlighting.

Eternally Awkward tracks the author's childhood, each chapter revealing "clues" in the form of embarrassing moments. This mystery of self-discovery delivers evidence that leads to the apprehension of the missing piece of her mental health picture—ADHD. Ride along on these ridiculous and, ultimately, very relatable stories of coming of age in the 1980s.

Contents

Introduction
to the
Discussion Guide

Welcome to the Eternally Expecting Discussion Guide! This interactive workbook has been thoughtfully designed to be compatible with Amy Liz Harrison's debut memoir and guide you on a journey of exploration and learning. Whether you're seasoned in recovery or sober-curious, this workbook is your dedicated companion.

Packed with engaging exercises and insightful prompts that correspond with each section of the book, this guide is here to offer a deeper understanding of both *Eternally Expecting* and yourself.

Prepare to embark on a transformative learning experience that will empower you to grasp concepts, apply principles, and achieve your recovery goals.

Introduction

Harrison says unity, recovery and service are the three legacies for 12 steppers. What thoughts does this evoke in you?

....
....
....
....
....
....
....
....
....
....
....
....
....
....
....
....
....
....

The three legacies Harrison mentions are in the shape of a triangle, with recovery as the foundation, and service and unity supporting each other. Share an example from your own life of some practices, structures or systems that fully rely on each other to function in a healthy manner.

....

....

....

....

....

....

....

....

....

....

....

....

....

....

....

....

....

Harrison mentions that she isn't responsible for the random first thoughts that present themselves to her brain, but she is in charge of the responses. Do you have a similar brain? Do you relate to this concept?

....

....

....

....

....

....

....

....

....

....

....

....

....

....

....

....

....

....

....

What does recovery mean to you in your own life?

....

....

....

....

....

....

What does service mean to you in your own life?

....

....

....

....

What does unity mean to you in your own life?

....

....

....

....

....

For parents, what were the most fulfilling parts of pregnancy and childbirth?

....

....

....

....

....

....

....

....

....

The most challenging parts of pregnancy and childbirth?

....

....

....

....

....

....

....

....

Do you have any experience with alcoholism in your own life or in your family?

....

....

....

....

....

....

....

....

....

....

....

....

....

....

....

....

....

....

YOUR THOUGHTS
JOURNAL

DATES: _____   MOOD: _____

....

....

....

....

....

....

....

....

....

....

....

....

GOALS

GRATITUDE LIST

CHAPTER 1

Conception

"The start of a journey to a new life."

Why were they staring at me? I wondered. How rude. "I hate people." I said out loud. In the background of my thoughts, I could hear my kids anxiously talking in raised tones from the backseat, my youngest daughter choking out a muffled cry.

My rear-view mirror displayed a Fourth of July-worthy display of red and blue lights flashing. Muddled as it was, my brain told my right foot to depress the brake pedal, which I did, with more force than I intended. Suddenly, I couldn't breathe. I needed air. Shakily, I pressed the button to lower the driver's window. My efforts to piece together what was occurring in real time were met with little success. Just then, a gust of wind rushed at me from the side, blowing my hair back. Discombobulated, it took a few seconds to discover I was staring at the silhouette of a backlit police officer.

Excerpt From: Amy Liz Harrison. "Eternally Expecting: A Mom of Eight Gives Birth to a Whole New Life...Her Own."

Chapter 1 is troubling, and clearly shows an ending is near. Why do you think Harrison called this chapter "The Beginning: The Start of a Journey to a New Life"?

....

....

....

....

....

....

....

....

....

....

....

....

....

....

....

....

....

Which emotions does Chapter 1 evoke in you? Why do you think that is?

It can be difficult to understand how someone can be so addicted to a substance that they would engage in the actions of this chapter. Do you understand? Why or why not?

....

....

....

....

....

....

....

....

....

....

....

....

....

....

....

....

....

If you were in Harrison's shoes what would you imagine you have done differently?

....

....

....

....

....

....

....

....

....

....

....

....

....

....

....

....

....

....

If you are willing, share an example of how darkness of some kind in your life led to a fresh start?

Harrison mentions she thought she could mold/shape her kids into who she wanted them to be, much like her Cabbage Patch Dolls in the 80s. From the perspective of a parent, do you think this is possible? Why or why not?

Now from a child's perspective, do you think it is possible for parents to mold/shape their kids into who they want them to be? Why or why not?

....

....

....

....

....

....

....

....

....

....

....

....

....

....

....

....

....

Did you as a child or do you now live inside your head, or have an internal dialogue? If so, do you ever wish you could shut it off? What are some ways you've tried to shut it off?

Do you think your childhood and adolescence helped shape who you are today? (Physical location of where you grew up, parents' goals and ambitions, concepts parents put value on, demographics/race, religious background, opportunities or lack thereof, etc;) Please share some ways these things impacted your development.

Harrison admits comparing her insides to others' outsides and wondering if she measured up. Can you relate? If so, how?

YOUR THOUGHTS
JOURNAL

DATES: MOOD:

....

....

....

....

....

....

....

....

....

....

GOALS   ## GRATITUDE LIST

CHAPTER 2

Embryonic Stage

"General growth pattern from fertilization to birth."

For Darla's birthday one year, The Planets took a memorable trip to her family's cabin in the lovely Pajaro Dunes, with views spanning from Santa Cruz to Monterey. Saturday morning, we piled into Darla's father's ATV and he took us four-wheeling all over the dunes. Dear reader, I'm talking no seatbelts, no helmets and certainly no cares in the world. We rocketed at speeds that were probably, in reality, completely cautious and safe, but felt like the Indiana Jones and the Temple of Doom ride at Disneyland. We rode standing up, hanging off the roll bar with one arm, flinging the other arm around in the sky as if we were on the steepest plunging dip of a roller coaster. We did not even consider for a hot minute that we should, at the very least, keep our limbs inside the vehicle. Sand and dirt flew out from beneath the powerful tires,and our small bodies were tossed side to side as the vehicle jolted and rocked. We laughed and screamed as the turbulent wind whipped our hair back, which was a welcome bonus, as this wasthe era of feathered 1980s hairstyles.

Excerpt From: Amy Liz Harrison. "Eternally Expecting: A Mom of Eight Gives Birth to a Whole New Life...Her Own."

Do you have any memories of feeling fearless as a child the way Harrison felt that day at the Pajaro Dunes in the Jeep?

Do you remember having a crew like the Planets? What do you remember about your schoolmates? What was your school experience like? How do you think it affected you?

....

....

....

....

....

....

....

....

....

....

....

....

....

....

....

....

....

....

Harrison mentions being ignored by Darla was the first time she felt rejection and emotional abandonment. Have you felt these emotions before? Do you remember the first time you felt these feelings? How did those emotions affect you?

Harrison mentions "light switch friends." Did you have any light switch friends growing up? Do you have any now? How did/ how do they affect you? How did you/do you deal with them?

The Aaron Piker incident left Harrison feeling out of the teachers' good graces and she realized she cared—a lot. Either as a child or currently, did/do you care what others thought/think? How does the opinion of others affect or not affect you today? If you're a former people pleaser, how did you get there?

The internal emotional chaos Harrison experienced was from her vantage point only, her perspective. Did you feel different from others as a child? If so, how? Did you question how others might view you, or wonder if your perception was off?

....

....

....

....

....

....

....

....

....

....

....

....

....

....

....

....

....

....

Figuring out what character she should play for you was a skill Harrison learned early in order to be liked and accepted. Can you relate? If so, how?

Do you remember having a crew like the Planets? If you were in school, what do you remember about your schoolmates? What was your school experience like? How do you think it affected you?

....

....

....

....

....

....

....

....

....

....

....

....

....

....

....

....

....

Harrison touches on escapism at the end of the chapter, mentioning she used food to escape her feelings. Share a few methods you've tried in an attempt to escape your feelings.

How have past attempts to escape feelings affected you?

Can you relate to Harrison's messy dance with the self-discovery that she was a "little much" for people, combined with pressure to perform appropriately? If so, how? And if not, what did you struggle with emotionally as a teen?

Harrison discusses wrestling with her faith and questioning God. Did you grow up with a faith? If so, which faith, and are you still a part of it?

If you're willing to share, what did you believe about a Higher Power as a child? How did it affect your life positively and negatively?

....

....

....

....

....

....

....

....

....

....

....

....

....

....

....

....

....

....

CHAPTER 2

If you're willing to share, what do you currently believe about a Higher Power/Spirituality?

CHAPTER 2

Harrison talks about learning "Impression Management" after the spring sing.

✔

What does this phrase mean to you?

....

✔

Did it or does it currently show up in your life?

....

✔

If so, how?

....

✔

If not, why do you think it doesn't?

....

YOUR THOUGHTS
JOURNAL

DATES: MOOD:

....
....
....
....
....
....
....
....
....
....
....
....

GOALS   ## GRATITUDE LIST

CHAPTER 3

Braxton Hicks

Painless, irregular contractions which don't promote the cervical changes necessary for the birthing process. Also known as "false labor."

Themes/Stories

Can you relate to Harrison's messy dance with the self-discovery that she was a "little much" for people, combined with pressure to perform appropriately? If so, how? And if not, what did you struggle with emotionally as a teen?

....
....
....
....
....
....
....
....
....
....
....
....
....

Harrison discusses wrestling with her faith and questioning God. Did you grow up with a faith? If so, which faith, and are you still a part of it?

....

....

....

....

....

....

....

....

....

....

....

....

....

....

....

....

....

If you're willing to share, what did you believe about a Higher Power as a child? How did it affect your life positively and negatively?

....

....

....

....

....

....

....

....

....

....

....

....

....

....

....

....

....

If you're willing to share, what do you currently believe about a Higher Power/Spirituality?

....
....
....
....
....
....
....
....
....
....
....
....
....
....
....
....
....
....

Where did you see yourself in the social lineup at school or in groups of other teens? Today, looking back, do you think your assessment was accurate? Why/why not?

CHAPTER 3

What were some of your first jobs? Looking back, how did they influence who you are today or add color to your life?

Do you remember your first drink?

....

....

....

....

....

....

....

....

What was it like/what happened?

....

....

....

....

....

....

....

....

Harrison talks about station wagons being the family vehicle of choice. Did your family of origin have a vehicle of choice or any peccadilloes or interesting idiosyncrasies unique to your family?

....

....

....

....

....

....

....

....

....

....

....

....

....

....

....

....

....

No one's life goes in a totally linear fashion, but in what ways has your life gone against the cultural norm or shown patterns of awkwardness or off-timing?

YOUR THOUGHTS
JOURNAL

DATES: MOOD:

....

....

....

....

....

....

....

....

....

....

....

....

GOALS   ## GRATITUDE LIST

CHAPTER 4

Contractions

"Rhythmic tightening pains of the uterus, becoming increasingly stronger and closer together to create cervical changes in preparation for birth."

""How about diapers?" *Prompted Mona.* "Raise your hand if you're using disposable. Now raise your hand if you're doing the environmentally friendly *cloth* diapers!" *Thankfully most everyone was in alignment on this one. Only two takers on the cloth. I sat in blissful ignorance of the sheer number of diapers I was going to be changing over the next few years and how much I was going to need the convenience of those disposable diapers."*

Excerpt From: Amy Liz Harrison. "Eternally Expecting: A Mom of Eight Gives Birth to a Whole New Life...Her Own."

Harrison talks about the women in the new baby class falling into categories: breastfeeding or bottle feeding and cloth or disposable diapers. Why do you suppose most women compare and compete with each other while men seem totally uninterested in each other's choices on parenting matters?

How have life events rocked your world in a negative manner? What phobias or issues have you developed as a result of certain life events? Have you worked through them? Have you ever felt that God, the universe, or a Higher Power was cruel or unjust? What were the circumstances?

....

....

....

....

....

....

....

....

....

....

....

....

....

....

....

....

....

....

Have you been through something that rocked the core of your spiritual foundation, and maybe even caused a deconstruction of faith? Have you switched religions or denied there is a God entirely?

....

....

....

....

....

....

....

....

....

....

....

....

....

....

....

....

....

....

Harrison mentions she was resentful at her husband. Who or what have you resented? How do you deal with resentments? How do you avoid getting more resentments?

....
....
....
....
....
....
....
....
....
....
....
....
....
....
....
....
....
....

Harrison talks about feeling balanced with Ava, who she thought was her final newborn, in the hospital. What does balance mean and look like to you?

When in your life do you feel balanced?

How does it impact you?

What do you do to achieve it?

How do you deal with stress and chaos in your life? How do you keep all the plates spinning?

Have you ever been jealous of your spouse, significant other, or best friend? Brave enough to share about it?

YOUR THOUGHTS
DAILY JOURNAL

DATES: MOOD:

....

....

....

....

....

....

....

....

....

....

GOALS   ## TO DO LIST

CHAPTER 5

Dilation & Effacement

"The enlarging and thinning of the cervix, caused by powerful contractions, during active labor."

"I began to put on those inner "victim" glasses and make everything about me. I mean, no one gave two craps if I took my kids to the store. In fact, it was as if I were invisible. Just another one of their 95% routine clientele: "white stay at home breeder-mom." If I sat in coach with my kids on a flight, not only did no one care, but passengers looked visibly annoyed. I imagined I could read their scowls… As they were convinced this was about to turn into the flight from hell, complete with the bonus gifts of screaming kids and maybe a food fight."

Excerpt From: Amy Liz Harrison. "Eternally Expecting: A Mom of Eight Gives Birth to a Whole New Life...Her Own."

Parents: Have you struggled with feeling like the crappiest parent on the block? In what ways?

....

....

....

....

....

....

....

....

....

....

....

....

....

....

....

....

....

Have you overcompensated to cover any insecurities or inadequacies? If you're willing, please share.

Have you ever thought everyone else had the handbook to life except for you?

....

....

....

....

....

....

....

....

....

....

....

....

....

....

....

....

....

....

....

Have you ever been completely perplexed by your inability to cease behaving or acting out in certain ways? If willing, please share.

Harrison mentions that she doesn't want anyone looking at her at the grocery store or on a flight with her children, yet she feels invisible as a human being. Can you relate? If so, how?

Harrison mentions putting on her inner victim glasses. Have you ever felt like a victim? How about a martyr? How did those viewpoints serve you? Do they still?

....

....

....

....

....

....

....

....

....

....

....

....

....

....

....

....

....

....

YOUR THOUGHTS
JOURNAL

DATES: MOOD:

....

....

....

....

....

....

....

....

....

....

GOALS

GRATITUDE LIST

CHAPTER 6

Transition

"The most intense part of labor, where contractions become curiously powerful and the mother doubts she can complete the birthing process. Also known as "the point of no return."

Can you relate to feeling like you were unraveling? If you're comfortable, share how you dealt with this or are currently handling this.

....

....

....

....

....

....

....

....

....

....

....

....

....

....

....

If you are willing, share about a time in your life when you were completely powerless and unable to regain control. AND What did you do about it?

....

....

....

....

....

....

....

....

....

....

....

....

....

....

....

....

....

Engaging in self destructive behaviors is often a sign of a deeper problem. For example, many suffer from PTSD, or postpartum depression. Can you relate to this at all? Or can you share an example of self sabotage? Or could you share a past experience?

....
....
....
....
....
....
....
....
....
....
....
....
....
....
....
....
....
....

What are some of the ways unmanageability shows up in your life?

....

....

....

....

....

....

....

....

....

....

....

....

....

....

....

....

....

....

How do you feel when things are unmanageable?

What are some of the best tools you've used to help free you from unmanageability?

....
....
....
....
....
....
....
....
....
....
....
....
....
....
....
....
....
....
....

YOUR THOUGHTS
JOURNAL

DATES: MOOD:

....

....

....

....

....

....

....

....

....

....

....

GOALS   ## GRATITUDE LIST

CHAPTER 7

Crowning

**"The point of largest stretching where birth is imminent.
Known in some cultures as "the ring of fire."**

How do you handle physical pain?

....

....

....

....

....

....

....

....

....

....

....

....

....

....

....

How do you generally handle emotional pain?

Can you talk about, even in general terms, the lowest point in your life? Self-inflicted or not. Could be something that happened, could be a death, accident, etc.

Can you describe your emotions at that low point?

....

....

....

....

....

....

....

....

....

....

....

....

....

....

....

....

....

What was the most helpful thing people said to you during that time?

....

....

....

....

....

....

....

....

....

....

....

....

....

....

....

....

....

....

What was the least helpful thing people said to you during that time?

What were some of the tools you considered using to help you feel better?

How did you handle it and what was the most helpful tool?

_____

_____

_____

_____

_____

_____

_____

_____

_____

_____

_____

_____

_____

_____

_____

_____

CHAPTER 7

If you had to go back to that place of pain, what would you do differently, if anything?

YOUR THOUGHTS
JOURNAL

DATES: MOOD:

....

....

....

....

....

....

....

....

....

....

GOALS   ## GRATITUDE LIST

CHAPTER 8

Delivery

"Infants are delivered into the world and let out their first cry. They have entered their new environment, experiencing the first moments of life outside the uterus."

"Over the next four weeks, Fred and I dumped out my junk drawer of denial and baggage and we began to sort through it, piece by piece, step by step. He taught me the power of rituals, which I had previously deemed a form of Satanic horoscope or fortune cookie-fruit from the devil himself, thanks to my Christian upbringing. He showed me how empowering it felt to clean up my own messes. Instead of shoving the closet door closed on all my skeletons, leaving it for the next poor unsuspecting victim to open, I started to take responsibility."

Excerpt From: Amy Liz Harrison. "Eternally Expecting: A Mom of Eight Gives Birth to a Whole New Life...Her Own."

Harrison talks about her shaman therapist, Fred, and her initial unwillingness to try new spiritual practices. Can you relate to resisting new concepts? Can you share an example?

....

....

....

....

....

....

....

....

....

....

....

....

....

....

....

....

....

Have you heard the term "Gift of Desperation" as an acronym for God? What does that mean to you?

....

....

....

....

....

....

....

....

....

....

....

....

....

....

....

....

....

....

Willing to share about a time where you've had that gift of desperation?

_____

_____

_____

_____

_____

_____

_____

_____

_____

_____

_____

_____

_____

_____

_____

_____

What emotions were evoked during that desperate time?

CHAPTER 8

Harrison said in order to recover she had tobecome teachable.

Can you relate?

....

Have you ever had to learn how to recoverfrom something in your life?

....

What helped you the most during that time?

....

Have you had many experiences with paradoxes? (Or things ending up to be the opposite of what they seemed to be at first?)

Like Harrison, have you ever been in a position where you just simply had to follow directions, even when you didn't understand what was going on?

....

....

....

....

....

....

....

....

....

....

....

....

....

....

....

....

....

CHAPTER 8

Can you relate to Harrison's description of coming home and having to make over her entire life? What were the circumstances and what did it feel like? Please share.

....

....

....

....

....

....

....

....

....

....

....

....

....

....

....

....

....

YOUR THOUGHTS
JOURNAL

DATES: MOOD:

....

....

....

....

....

....

....

....

....

....

....

GOALS   ## GRATITUDE LIST

CHAPTER 9

Cutting the Umbilical Cord

"The official separation of the infant from their former supply of nutrients."

Harrison describes her life taking a sharp unexpected turn with her 5th pregnancy. At what times in your life have you experienced life's surprises?

Can you describe a time when you found yourself starting all over again in your life? (Maybe a move, a death, new job, etc.)

Harrison became closely connected to 12 step members who she would have never crossed paths with if not for recovery. Can you share about a time you received valuable support from an unlikely source?

....

....

....

....

....

....

....

....

....

....

....

....

....

....

....

....

....

If you've had an "opposites attract" experience, can you share what connected you to the other person?

....

....

....

....

....

....

....

....

....

....

....

....

....

....

....

....

....

Have you ever experienced a "second chance?" in parenting? In life? Please share.

Harrison describes getting comfortable with being
uncomfortable. Can you relate? Describe that situation.

Harrison describes becoming more comfortable over time with things that previously scared her, like public speaking. Have you had any similar experiences you can share?

YOUR THOUGHTS
JOURNAL

DATES: MOOD:

....

....

....

....

....

....

....

....

....

....

....

GOALS   ## GRATITUDE LIST

CHAPTER 10

Afterbirth

"The womb begins a process of self-cleaning, expelling materials no longer benefitting the infant. Additionally the infant must learn the ongoing process of seeking and ingesting nutrients so they can grow."

Harrison talks about her near-death experience with Myocarditis and Heart Failure and getting an Internal cardiac Defibrillator implant. Have you had a health crisis that has brought you to your knees? What was it?

....

....

....

....

....

....

....

....

....

....

....

....

....

If you have had a health crisis, what were the tools that helped you (or are helping you) through that time?

What mindsets did you have to let go of?

Looking back over the course of your life, have you grown the most when things have been comfortable and fun? Or painful and challenging? Explain.

Have you experienced a reconstruction of faith? Brave enough to share about it?

Harrison weaves the strength of her commitment to her kids throughout the book. She also describes how her husband Andrew never left her side, though she questioned all her relationships during her darkest days. Can you share a time when you questioned whether you would have the support you needed?

....
....
....
....
....
....
....

Did you get that support?

....
....
....
....
....
....
....

Harrison shared how her good friend and former drinking buddy, Jen, ended up staying by her side. Have you had unexpected gifts or relationships arise out of troublesome times? Discuss. Harrison shared how her good friend and former drinking buddy, Jen, ended up staying by her side. Have you had unexpected gifts or relationships arise out of troublesome times? Discuss.

Sometimes our worst decisions can turn into our best treasures. The ripple effect of Harrison's recovery is passed on to the next generation of Harrisons because of her family's forgiveness, and because she recovered out loud. In what ways have you let your past become your greatest asset?

YOUR THOUGHTS
JOURNAL

DATES: MOOD:

....
....
....
....
....
....
....
....
....
....
....

GOALS   ## GRATITUDE LIST

EPILOGUE

Motherhood and sobriety transformed Harrison. Can you relate?
Do you have a significant life event that transformed you?

Being present is a gift that Harrison didn't have in her alcoholism. Because she has it now, she is able to appreciate it and see the importance in feeling her feelings and experiencing life on life's terms. How has being present affected you?

Harrison explains how some life events are so powerful, you're not the same person you were before. Can you relate to this?

Has Eternally Expecting encouraged you to pursue your journey differently in any way? Examples: pursue personal growth, try getting sober, have some more babies?
(Just kidding about the last one.)

YOUR THOUGHTS
JOURNAL

DATES: MOOD:

....

....

....

....

....

....

....

....

....

....

GOALS

GRATITUDE LIST